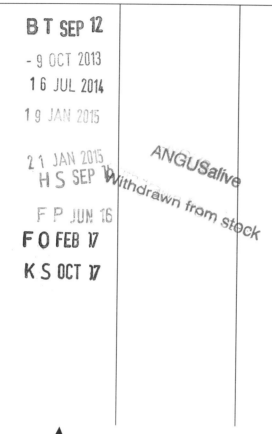
From the collection
of
Maureen Dawson of Arbroath

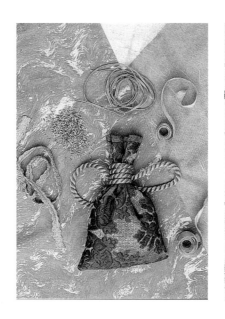

BEAUTIFUL
HOMEMADE
PRESENTS

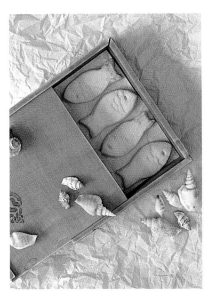

Over 35 projects with step-by-step instructions

JULIET BAWDEN

COLLINS & BROWN

First published in Great Britain in 1998
by Collins & Brown Limited
London House
Great Eastern Wharf
Parkgate Road
London SW11 4NQ

10 9 8 7 6 5 4 3 2 1

British Library Cataloguing-in-Publication Data:
A catalogue record for this book is available
from the British Library.

ISBN 1 85585 499 6 (paperback edition)

Editor: Patricia Burgess
Art Director: John Strange
Designer: Judith Robertson
Editorial Director: Pippa Rubinstein

Reproduction by Pixel Tech Prepress Pre Ltd,
Singapore
Printed and bound in Slovenia
by Mladinska knjiga Tiskarna d.d.

Contents

Introduction 6

Introduction

I was delighted when I was asked to write this book on homemade presents, as I love both giving and receiving them. The challenge was to come up with ideas which were beautiful and original, yet not difficult to achieve. Some of the gifts are made from scratch, but many are shop-bought and then customized to make something special – an original one-off gift. For example, terracotta pots with a relief design can be given a coat of paint or embellished with cabochons, or small flowering plants can be dug up from the garden and presented in pretty baskets or white china bowls. With just a few imaginative touches, the mundane can be made visually pleasing.

Presents in this book cater for people of all ages, from babies to adults, and none require more than basic skills – indeed some are simplicity itself. There are gifts for special occasions, such as birthdays and Christmas, and ideas for gifts of flowers and food that can be used for any occasion.

Although the book is arranged in categories, many of the gifts are interchangeable, as a Christmas present might be suitable for a birthday, or a present for the home may be given at Christmas. This book is simply packed with ideas, and includes numerous variations on the basic themes.

I hope you will have as much fun making and giving these gifts as I have.

Juliet Bawden

Birthday Presents

As birthday gifts are given to people of all ages and tastes, here are a selection of ideas that can be adapted to suit anyone.

A découpaged frame may be just the present for that impossible person who already has everything!

Decorated flowerpots are a fun and easy gift idea, and can be given to almost anyone. They can also be used as candleholders, like those shown here, or filled with sweets, bath items, or packets of seeds for a keen gardener.

A brooch is a piece of jewellery that can be made in either a masculine or feminine style. Alternatively, using the same design and method of construction, the brooch can be made into a tie-pin or cuff-links for a man, or a pair of earrings for a woman. The motif – perhaps a car, a plane, a dog, a cat or flowers – can reflect the interests of the person receiving the present.

A wrap is probably a present for women only, but it is the most wonderful gift as it can be customized to suit the woman for whom it is made, and is also ageless. Choose a wild and wacky colour combination for an extrovert friend, or a mixture of sumptuous silks and satins for someone who attends grand occasions.

Beeswax candles make a lovely and aromatic present, suitable for almost anyone. They can also be decorated with beads, pins, ribbons and dried flowers for friends with more elaborate tastes.

Variations

You can découpage a frame, as above, using almost any type of paper. Why not colour photocopy the picture you want to put in the frame and use it as découpage so that the frame echoes the picture?

Découpaged Frames

Découpage is a very easy way of personalizing
a gift. For example, stamps arranged around a frame
are a good idea for a philatelist. You do not need to use originals; instead, photocopy them,
then cut and stick the photocopies onto the frame. A letter, handwritten message,
drawing or other paper memento can be used for decorative purposes.
The small wooden frame here has been decorated by first staining it in tea to give it
an aged look, then découpaging with photocopies of letters from friends. The letters used here were full
of drawings, which have been used to decorate the frame, and the major drawing – a portrait
of the sender – has been given pride of place inside the frame.

1 Photocopy the source material, and then artificially age it by rubbing it with damp tea bags until it is thoroughly stained.

2 Rip up the découpage pieces and arrange them to fit around the frame. Stick into place initially with mounting putty until satisfied with the 'finished' appearance.

You will need

Sources of découpage
(stamps, letters, magazine
pictures, wallpaper, etc.)
Scissors
Damp tea bags
Wide, flat frame
Mounting putty (Blu-tack)
Glue
Polyurethane varnish
Paintbrush

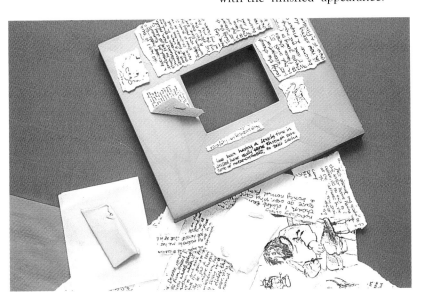

3 Remove the mounting putty and glue the pieces into position. After the glue has dried, apply several coats of clear polyurethane varnish over the découpaged surface. Leave to dry between coats.

Decorated Flowerpots

 *Flowerpots can look very pretty
when personalized with hand-painting.
Some flowerpots have a rim which can be decorated
by painting it in a contrasting colour, or by gluing on cabochons or
shaped sequins. Flowerpots may be made from other materials, such
as china, and may have a raised-surface design such as a sun,
cherub or fleur de lys, which can also be painted in
contrasting colours for an attractive effect.*

You will need

*Flowerpots of various types
(plain or with raised motifs)
Emulsion or acrylic paints,
in bright colours
Paintbrush
Gold paint
Candles*

2 When the contrasting paint colour has dried, carefully paint in the raised pattern with gold paint, making sure the lines are as neat as possible. Paint on extra coats of gold to brighten the colour if necessary, then leave to dry.

3 Paint the rim of the pot in gold and leave to dry. Insert candles, if you wish.

1 Paint the outside of the flowerpot first with emulsion or acrylic paint, leaving the raised pattern and the top rim unpainted. Leave to dry.

Variations

*Paint the rim and outside
of plain terracotta flowerpots
in contrasting colours
and leave to dry. When the
paint has dried, glue on
cabochons, stones
or sequins.*

Heart Brooch

This opulent brooch is made from velvet which has been edged with gold metallic thread and beads. This has been done using a zigzag attachment on a sewing machine, but if you don't have one, you can achieve the same results by hand-sewing a very close blanket stitch. Although I have chosen to make a heart shape, you can use the same technique to create any motif you desire, such as a flag, personal initial or animal design.
You may also want to make an attractive card with a frame on which to mount and present the brooch. The card can be made more interesting by using découpage techniques (see page 11) or by hand-painting. A simple card for mounting the brooch is included in the instructions here.

You will need

Iron-on heavyweight
interfacing
Small scrap of red velvet
Iron and ironing board
Card
Pencil
Scissors
Fabric marker pen
Sewing machine
(or needle and thread)
Gold thread
Beading needle
Invisible thread
Bugle beads
Small gold beads
Large glass bead
Larger gold bead
Strong adhesive
Brooch-back
Frame
Small sticker

1 Press two or three pieces of the interfacing onto the wrong side of a piece of red velvet 7 x 7 cm (2¾ x 2¾ in) with a hot iron. Make a card template of the heart shape and mark this on the stiffened velvet piece. Work a straight stitch along the marked line.

2 Cut out the shape, leaving an extra 2 mm (⅛ in) space beyond the stitched line.

14

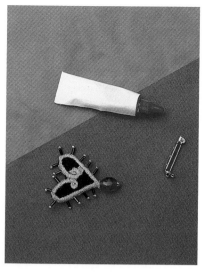

3 Iron a piece of iron-on interfacing onto the back of the heart shape to stabilize it. Then use gold thread to work a zigzag stitch around it, enclosing the raw edges.

4 In the gold edge, make a stitch with the beading needle and invisible thread. Thread the needle through a bugle bead, then a gold bead and back again. Make a stitch along the gold edge and repeat.

5 Glue the metal brooch-back into position on the wrong side of the heart. Leave to dry until firmly attached.

6 Cut a piece of card 20 x 15 cm (8 x 6 in) and score in half lengthways. Find a frame, place the card in the centre and glue into position. Pass the sticker through the clasp of the brooch, with the sticky side towards you, then stick the brooch firmly to the card.

Variations

The technique used to make this brooch can be used with many other shapes – in fact, you may find it easier to work with geometric shapes.
Try using squares and circles, adding beads for decoration. Sew initials, if you wish, or satin stitch lines to create an image, like the flag on page 15.

Beeswax Candles

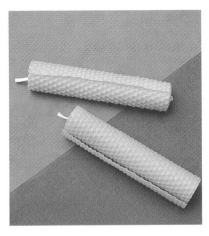 Beeswax candles can be expensive to buy,
but are easy and inexpensive to make. Beeswax
can be bought in sheet form in a variety of colours, widths and thicknesses.
As long as it is fairly fresh, it is pliable and easy to roll into candles.
Beeswax smells delicious either when lit or unlit.

You will need

Beeswax
Wicks
Beeswax sheets
Dried rosebud heads
for decoration

2 Continue rolling to the end of the beeswax, then gently press the edge down to secure the candle and also to protect it from unravelling.

3 Add a pretty touch to the candle by pinning dried rosebuds around the base of it.

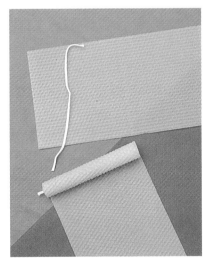

1 Melt some beeswax and dip the wick into it, then leave to dry (this is optional, as you can also use the wick undipped). Lay the wick on the wax sheet and gently begin to roll the sheet around it.

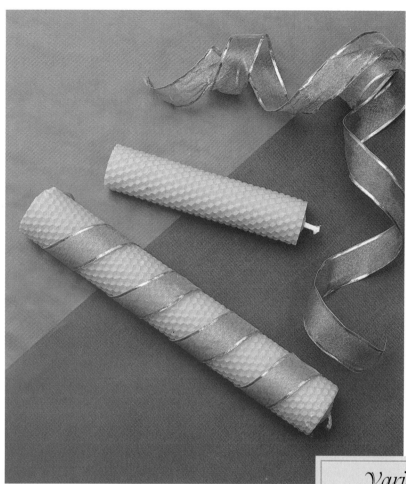

Variations

Another way of decorating
beeswax candles is to wind a
pretty coloured ribbon around
it or, using pins, to stick beads
into the candle at evenly spaced
intervals. Unwind the ribbon
before lighting the candle.

Wrap

A wrap is a present that can be given to a woman of any age. The wrap designed here is reversible and a layer of wadding is sandwiched between the two fabrics for warmth. The toile (pattern) for the wrap is first made from calico. To work out the amount of material you will need, place it around your neck – it should hang down on either side as far as your knees. The amount will need adjusting, depending on whether the recipient is taller or shorter than you. The width should be approximately 45 cm (18 in).

You will need

Approximately 2.5 m (2½ yd) each of calico, red velvet and pink silk
Fabric marker pen
Scissors
Approximately 2.5m (2½ yd) of medium-weight wadding
Dressmaker's pins
Sewing machine
Needle and thread

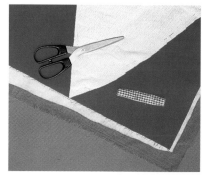

2 Place the wadding on the pink silk and the red velvet on top. Pin the calico pattern on top and cut out.

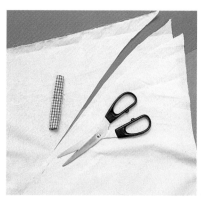

1 Cut a piece of calico to the length required. Draw a quarter circle on one end and cut out. Fold the fabric in half and cut another quarter circle at the other end to round off the back corners. Try the fabric around your shoulders, with the straight side forward, and adjust to fit. The calico forms the pattern for the wrap.

3 Sew the pink silk to the wadding around the edge, right side up. Around the circular edge, sew the red velvet, right side down, on top of the pink silk. Then sew from either end of the straight edge, leaving enough room in the centre to turn through, and remove all the pins. Turn right side out and close the gap with slipstitches.

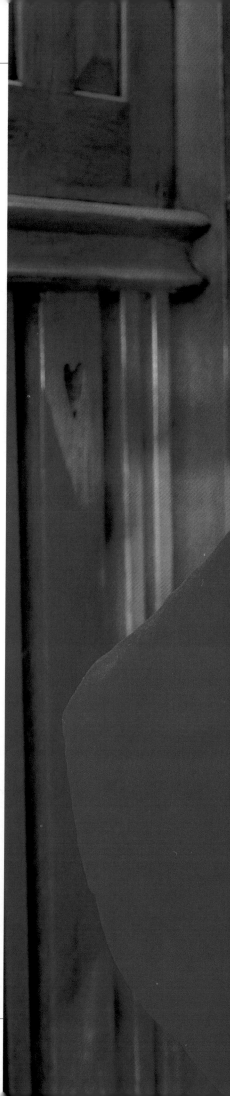

Nature's Gifts

Flowers and plants are lovely traditional gifts, but too often they are presented without any originality. I have therefore dreamed up some innovative ideas to transform floral gifts using only basic ingredients.

Each season is represented in these floral gifts, and included are also dried-flower arrangements, for example, a fragrant wreath made from dried lavender, for the times when you can't get fresh flowers.

Hyacinths may be planted hydroponically (without soil) in glass containers so that the bulb and the roots are left visible. You can also add pieces of dried, varnished fruit to hyacinths planted in soil for decoration.

Snowdrops are very pretty, but you can augment their natural beauty by putting them into white china or glass dishes. Colourful crocuses are one of the first signs of spring, and can be planted in fabric-lined baskets to add cheer to a present for a friend or relative.

Topiary trees look wonderful and you may be surprised at how easy they are to make.

A floral swag can be made by following the basic instructions given. You can vary this easily by putting in whatever flowers are in season or those that appeal to your own colour sense.

A plain basket can be made into an original gift by gluing nuts around the rim and applying gold gilt wax over the entire basket to give it a golden lustre.

Hyacinths

Winter can seem grim without the flowering beauty and scents of warmer seasons – thank goodness for hyacinths, which can be planted at intervals throughout the autumn for fragrant flowering from Christmas onwards. As a simple gift idea, they can be planted in pretty baskets and covered in moss, or for a more unusual and stylish option, they can be planted hydroponically (without soil). Here hyacinth bulbs have been planted in clear glass containers with star fruit pieces arranged around the inside of the container for an extra imaginative touch.

You will need

Hyacinth bulbs
Large plant pot
Potting compost
Large clear glass containers
Star fruit, dried and varnished
(use a clear varnish)
Sharp knife

1 Plant the hyacinth bulbs in a large plant pot. Make sure the bulbs are kept moist and in a cool, dark place. Allow them to grow for a couple of weeks until they begin to bud.

2 Water and check the flowers regularly until they have grown enough to be given as a gift.

3 Slice the star fruit, allow to dry, then varnish. Place in a row around the bottom of the glass container. Carefully add the potting compost, taking care not to get the compost between the glass and the fruit. Then pack the soil until the star fruit slices are covered.

4 Transfer the hyacinths to the glass container. Place more star fruit in a second row around the container and fill it up with compost. The hyacinth roots should be buried quite deep.

Note You may need help when pouring the soil over the star fruit in order to keep it neat.

Snowdrops in White China

Snowdrops are a very simple but pretty gift.
They flower for only a short period of time,
so make the most of them by presenting them in pieces of white china that can be grouped
together attractively on a table or windowsill. Old-fashioned jelly moulds and jugs make
unusual containers, as do jam jars or modern sugar bowls.

You will need

Two or three old-fashioned
white china jelly moulds
Potting compost
2 or 3 plants per jelly mould
(if snowdrops are
not in season, choose other
small flowers such as
forget-me-nots)
Moss (optional)

1 Wash and dry the jelly moulds.
Place a thin layer of potting compost
at the bottom of each mould.

2 Gently place two or three plants in the container and press down with your fingertips.

3 Top up with some more potting compost or soil. If you have any moss, this can look pretty laid on top of the soil. Arrange the pots to stand together in a group.

Topiary Tree

This very simple and elegant topiary tree can be made quickly and easily with a few specialist materials. The foliage of the tree is a sphere of florist's foam which has been covered in kiln-dried moss. The trunk is created by tying small twigs together to form a base for the moss ball. This tree is a wonderful present for anyone, especially for those who love plants but are not blessed with green fingers.

You will need

4–6 straight twigs or
cinnamon sticks
Secateurs
Linen string
Florist's foam (available in
blocks, cones or spheres)
Glue gun
Kiln-dried moss
Tacks or German
(U-shaped) pins
Scissors
Terracotta pot
Soil
Shiny bead-headed pins
Star-shaped sequins

2 Carefully push the trunk into the foam, taking care that the sphere does not crumble. Remove the trunk, apply glue to the hole that has been made, then push the trunk back into it. Allow to dry.

1 Cut the twigs or cinnamon sticks to the same length. Bind them together with the linen string to form the trunk of the topiary tree.

Variations

You can be even more adventurous and attach two spheres together, one on top of the other, to imitate the appearance of a hedge sculpture. Once the basic method is mastered, the possibilities are endless. Conical topiary trees are ideal for Christmas – pin beads and other colourful decorations around the tree to give it a festive feel.

3 Carefully arrange the moss around the foam, securing it in place with tacks or German pins. You will find that this is difficult to do with one piece of moss, so cut it up and then fill in all the spaces. Smooth the moss down firmly.

4 Place the tree in the terracotta pot and fill with soil. Pat down firmly to support the tree. Decorate the tree as you wish.

Floral Swag

This gift is perfect for many special occasions, especially christenings and weddings, where it can be hung on the door to welcome people into the festivities. It is a simple idea, using chicken wire as the base to hang the flowers from.

You will need

Length of chicken wire long enough to hang across door, mantlepiece or table, plus allowance for the curve of the swag
Florist's foam block
Selection of foliage and flowers
Florist's wire
Florist's tape
Secateurs
Ribbon

1 Cut the chicken wire to length, then roll into a long tube. Cut the florist's foam to fit inside the rolled wire, then secure the tube with florist's wire.

2 Begin to insert the larger flowers into spaces in the chicken wire. There is no real order in which you should arrange them, although a swag looks better if it is weighted more in the centre so that it hangs well. Push the flower stems into the foam and secure with florist's wire and tape.

3 Fill the gaps between the large flowers with smaller flowers, buds and foliage cut to fit the spaces.

Variations

*Why not make a wedding garland as a gift for the bride and groom. For summer, use fresh small rosebuds in a colour that matches the bride's bouquet. It could be hung from the front of the banqueting table or from a mantlepiece.
In winter replace the fresh flowers with dried ones.*

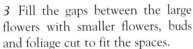

4 Keep adding foliage and flowers until you have completely covered the wire and the foam.

5 Finish off by attaching matching ribbons at either end of the chicken wire so you can hang the swag up.

Nut Basket

*The idea behind this gift is to cover a
basket in delectable nuts in their shells.
The shells have been gilded with wax to make them stand out in relief
against the weave of the basket.*

You will need

*Selection of walnuts, brazil
nuts and hazelnuts in
their shells
Gold gilt wax
Soft cloth
Glue gun
Large shallow basket, with
dark-coloured wickerwork*

1 Rub the nuts with gold wax, using
a soft cloth to wipe away the excess.
Don't cover the nuts too thickly or
too evenly.

2 Heat up the glue gun and attach
the larger nuts at random points
around the outside of the basket.

3 Fill in the spaces left with the
smaller nuts, and continue adding
nuts until you achieve a suitably
decorative look.

Crocuses in a Basket

Flowers are always a beautiful
and welcome gift. These yellow and
purple crocuses, with their refreshing fragrance and bright colours,
are ideal for cheering someone up and lifting their spirits. Make the
gift an absolute surprise by leaving a basket of them on the
recipient's doorstep so that when they open the door
on a miserable Monday morning they are
faced with instant sunshine.

You will need

Small basket with a handle
Plastic sheeting (a transparent
plastic bag will suffice)
Scissors
Needle and thread
Potting compost
Crocuses

1 Measure the inside of the basket and cut the plastic sheeting to fit around the inside, leaving a seam allowance. Then, using a needle and cotton thread, sew the sheeting into the basket, securing the top around the inside edge of the basket.

2 Fill the lined basket with potting compost. As crocuses tend to droop, they will need to be supported as much as possible, so pack the basket very full of compost and make sure the holes for the flowers reach right down to the bottom of the basket. Plant the flowers close together and pat down the surrounding compost.

Variations

For a dramatic finishing
touch, tie huge bows of
brightly coloured ribbons
to the handles of the
basket or around
the base.

Lavender Wreath

A fragrant wreath made from lavender looks lovely and smells divine. It can be hung on a door to give a subtle waft of lavender fragrance as you walk by, or suspended in a linen cupboard to scent sheets and towels.

You will need

Bunches of fresh lavender (the amount depends on how large you want the wreath to be)
Small twig wreath, shop-bought or home-made (see page 96)
Fine florist's wire or string
Scissors

2 Cut the stems off the lavender, within 5 cm (2 in) of the string so they won't protrude too far when attached to the wreath. Make up as many bunches as you think you will need to cover the wreath.

4 Continue adding the lavender bunches around the circle, securing firmly and ensuring that each time a new bunch is added, the exposed stems of the previous bunch are completely hidden. Continue until the circle is covered with lavender and no stems are visible.

1 Divide the lavender into bunches containing 10–15 flower heads. Tie them together tightly with wire or string, leaving quite long ends so the bunches can be tied to the wreath.

3 Starting at the bottom of the twig circle, bind a bunch of lavender to it using the long ends of its wire or string. Lay the next bunch slightly over the first, with the flower heads covering the exposed stems, and secure in place as before.

Variations

A charming rural appearance can be given to the basic lavender wreath by inserting a few ears of bright yellow corn. Wreaths, however, can be made from many other things. Most dried flowers look wonderful in circular arrangements: try dried roses and a variety of dried foliage, even dried fruit slices. They can be attached to the wreath with either florist's wire or a glue gun.

Gifts for the Home

 This section covers the kinds of gifts that you would normally give to friends or family members as housewarming or wedding presents. They are gifts that can be adapted to suit the décor in their homes or to suit their individual taste.

Simple ideas, such as lavender bags and scented herbal sachets, are always welcome presents. Small, pretty and fragrant, they are suitable for any room in the home.

Two ideas for homemade lampshades are included in this section; both are unusual, but are simple to make and effective, especially as gifts for friends who have just finished decorating their home and have yet to accessorize.

The miniature chest of drawers is an unusual gift, since furniture is not normally given as a present, but as this is tiny, it is ideal for knick-knacks. The chest of drawers in this section has been painted with a particular colour theme, but it can easily be adapted for a child's room, or the motifs can be made to look more descriptive to show what is kept in the drawers.

Finally, there are examples of boxes which have been decorated using simple techniques such as crackle glazing and découpage. The boxes can be given as gifts in themselves, or used as pretty containers for gifts, and can then be re-used for attractive storage after they have been opened.

Decoy Duck Découpaged Box

Boxes of all shapes and sizes can be beautiful gifts in themselves or used as containers for gifts. This plain Shaker box has been transformed by simple découpage, using colour photocopies of decoy ducks that have been carefully cut out, then glued and varnished onto the surface to look as though the ducks have been painted on. You can use your favourite images to decorate a box.

You will need

Plain wooden
or cardboard box
Gold and brown acrylic paint
Paintbrushes
Good quality colour
photocopies of images
you wish to use
Mounting putty (Blu-tack)
PVA glue
Craft knife
Découpage varnish

2 If the images you want to use are in a book, colour photocopy them, reducing or enlarging them to the size required. Carefully cut out the images using a craft knife.

4 Allow the glue to dry, ensuring that there are no air bubbles in the glued-down images. If there are, make a tiny slit in the image with a craft knife and push out the bubble.

Varnish the box with four to six layers of découpage varnish, leaving each layer to dry completely before applying the next. The varnish looks milky when applied, but it will dry clear.

1 Paint the box with gold and brown acrylic paint, mixing the paints on the box, to give it a streaked and dappled effect.

3 Arrange the ducks or other images around the box and lid and stick them in position with mounting putty (Blu-tack). Once you are happy with the arrangement, stick them on properly with PVA glue.

Variation

Boxes of all shapes and sizes can be découpaged with any type of paper – from photocopied images to foil and tissue paper. Follow the technique described on this page, positioning the découpaged pieces first with mounting putty, before gluing permanently in position.

The pictures of ducks shown left and below can be colour photocopied and used to découpage your chosen box.

Lavender Bags

These little bags, filled here with lavender, are very simple to make, and can be used for a variety of purposes. They can, for example, be used instead of gift wrap, or for holding little trinkets. As they are so easy to make, you can make them bigger or smaller to hold things of different sizes.

You will need

Pieces of rich fabric: satin, brocade, silk, etc.
Dressmaker's scissors
Sewing machine
Matching thread
Pinking shears
Lavender flowers
Ribbon or fabric tie

1 Work out how large you want the bag to be, then cut out a piece of fabric twice that size lengthways. The best shape is rectangular, so the piece should be a long rectangle.

2 Fold the fabric in half lengthways and sew up the sides with right sides together. Using the pinking shears, give the opening edges a nice finish, or if the material frays, turn the edges under and hem them down neatly. Turn the bag right side out.

3 Stuff the bag with the lavender, or put your gift inside and tie it tightly, using a matching ribbon or tie made from a strip of the same fabric.

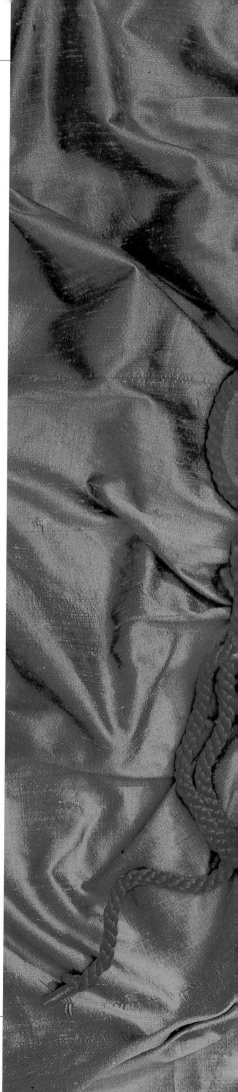

Threaded Lampshade

Plain lampshades are always useful gifts,
but if you prefer, they can be embellished to
add extra interest. If a friend has moved or redecorated recently,
you could decorate a lampshade to match the new décor. While it is difficult to be
sure of everyone's taste, you can hardly go wrong with a simple cream or white shade
that has been threaded with a ribbon in the colour of the recipient's décor.

You will need

Tape measure or ruler
Plain cream or white
coolie-shaped lampshade
Pencil
Hole puncher
Ribbon

1 Measure and mark off every 4 cm
(1½ in) along the lower edge of the
shade with a pencil. Then measure
and mark off every 3 cm (1¼ in)
along the top edge of the shade.

2 Using a hole puncher, make holes
at the points marked off. Punch just
above the rim seam, about 2 cm
(¾ in) in from the edge. You may
have to use a little force to punch
right through the shade material.

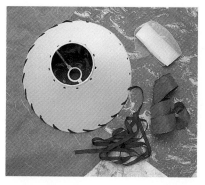

3 Starting at the back of the shade,
thread the ribbon through the holes
as if you were overstitching. Do the
lower edge first, then thread the
ribbon through the top edge.

Variations

Once the holes have
been punched in the shade,
the variations on how to
thread and embellish it are
countless. Instead of
running the ribbon straight
through the holes, thread it in a
blanket or cross-stitch fashion.
Alternatively, thread it from
the top holes to the lower holes
across the entire lampshade.
Braid, cord or thick
thread can be used
instead of ribbon.

Leaf Silhouette Paper Lampshade & Gilded Base

Transform a shop-bought lampshade and base from mundane household objects into attractive gifts. The idea behind this project is to cut out paper motifs and glue them onto the inside of the shade so that when the light is turned on, the shapes appear silhouetted against the shade.

You will need

Textured parchment lampshade
Matching lamp base
Tape measure
Textured, heavy white paper
Pencil
Cutting mat
Craft knife
Monting putty (Blu-tack)
PVA
Gold gilt wax
Soft cloth

1 Measure the height of the shade and draw simple leaf shapes in smallish sizes on the paper; make sure they will fit within the shade.

2 Place the paper on a cutting mat, and cut out the shapes using a sharp craft knife to get a good outline. Draw a 'vein' through the middle of the leaf, cut around it, then remove the middle section.

3 When you have cut enough leaves to fit around the whole shade, arrange them attractively inside it, using mounting putty (Blu-tack) so you will be able to move them around if you wish.

4 Once you are satisfied with the arrangement, use PVA glue to stick the leaves in position.

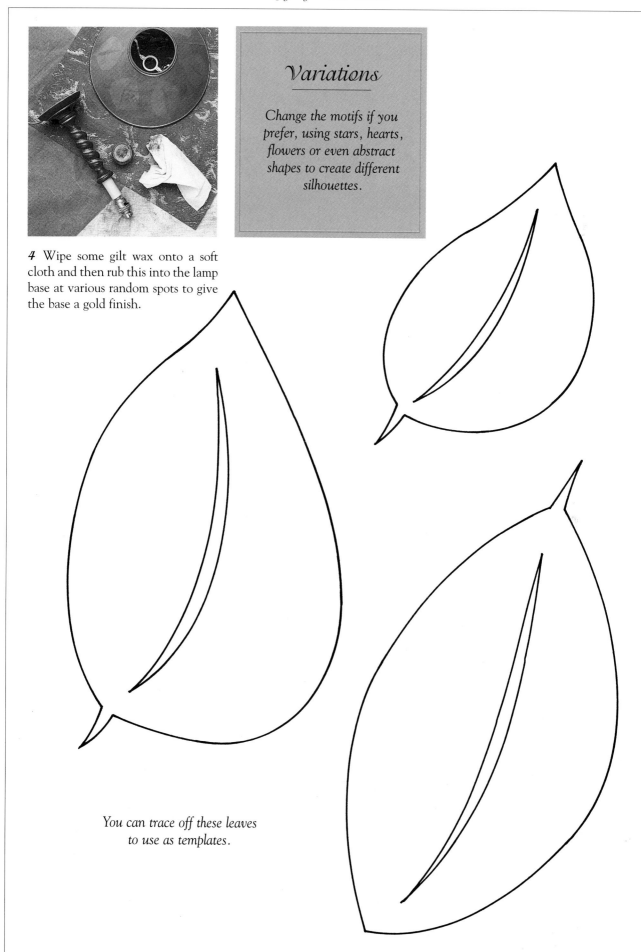

Variations

Change the motifs if you prefer, using stars, hearts, flowers or even abstract shapes to create different silhouettes.

4 Wipe some gilt wax onto a soft cloth and then rub this into the lamp base at various random spots to give the base a gold finish.

You can trace off these leaves to use as templates.

Herbal Sachet Bags

These very simple drawstring bags make fragrant sachets in which to fill with herbs, dried flowers or pot pourri. Use simple fabrics like gingham, calico or even hessian to achieve a Shaker look. Place in drawers or hang them up in cupboards to allow the fragrances of lavender, oregano and other flowers and herbs to fill the air.

You will need

Small piece of gingham, calico or hessian fabric
Tape measure
Pencil
Scissors
Sewing machine
Thread
Iron and ironing board
Needle
Green embroidery thread
Fragrant herbs

1 Cut the gingham into a rectangle measuring 42 x 14 cm (16 ½ x 5 ½ in) to form the main body of the bag. Then carefully cut a 4 x 40 cm (1 ½ x 16 in) gingham strip to make the drawstring.

2 Fold the main piece of fabric in half lengthways, then sew down the two long edges. Now fold down the top edges by 5 cm (2 in) and press.

Sew across the fold 4 cm (1½ in) down, then sew another line 1 cm (½ in) below the previous line. This will make a channel for the drawstring. Unpick the side seam between the two lines of stitching.

3 Fold the gingham strip in half lengthways and turn down the raw edges. Press, then sew along the open edges. Cut the drawstring in half and feed one half through each channel, using a safety pin to guide the drawstring. Push the ends through to the right side and knot.

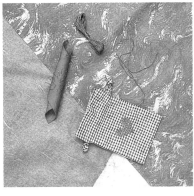

4 Turn the bag right side out, and draw a heart on the front of the bag. Cross stitch the heart pattern using green embroidery thread.

Variation

Light, translucent fabrics, such as broderie anglaise and voile, can be used so that the herbs show through and emit their fragrance even more effectively.

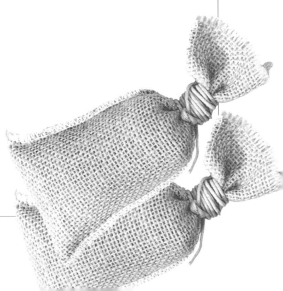

Hand-painted Miniature Chest of Drawers

This miniature chest of drawers was bought unpainted. It has been given washes in various shades of blue and then tiny motifs have been painted onto it. The chest is quite attractive without a paint finish, so you could just paint on motifs without giving it a wash, or even stamp or sponge paint onto the drawers.

You will need

Acrylic or emulsion paints in various soft shades of blue, mauve or another colour
Paintbrushes – one thick and one fine
Miniature wooden chest of drawers
Old rag
Pencil
Ruler

1 Dilute the paint colour that you are going to use on the chest (one part paint to two parts water), then quickly paint a wash of it over the chest. While it is still wet, rub the colour into the grain of the wood with the old rag.

2 This chest has six drawers, and each pair has been painted in different colours – mauve, sky blue and medium blue. They were also painted in the same manner as the chest. While the wash is still wet, rub the colour into the grain of the wood with a rag.

3 Once the paint on the drawers is dry, draw on the motifs – squares, oblongs, squiggles as used here, or anything you choose – with a pencil. The squares and oblongs were measured and spaced with a ruler to give an even appearance.

4 Using a fine paintbrush and undiluted paint in the same colours that were used as a wash, fill in the pencilled outlines. Make sure you paint carefully over any visible pencil lines.

Crackle-glazed Découpaged Box

 Crackle glazing is a very quick way of ageing an object and adds fun to your gift-making. Here, a gift box is découpaged using a greeting-card copy of an ancient painting, which is then further 'antiqued' with crackle glaze. Crackle-glaze kits are available in craft shops and consist of lacquer, gold size and a crackle medium. A couple of layers of lacquer are painted onto the surface, then the gold size is applied over the lacquer and left until sticky. Lastly, the crackle medium is applied in a thin coat and left to dry overnight, after which the cracks will have appeared. This process works because the elements have different drying times, and they react when one layer is painted over another.

You will need

Round box
Gold acrylic paint
Paintbrushes
Photocopied images
Scissors
Cutting mat
Craft knife
PVA glue
Crackle-glaze kit,
which includes lacquer,
gold size, crackle glaze and
Raw umber oil paint
Kitchen paper
Polyurethane varnish

2 Cut out the chosen images to fit onto the box, using a craft knife to ensure a sharp, clean outline. Glue the cut-outs into position on the painted box and rub over each one with your finger to remove any air bubbles or wrinkles.

4 When the lacquer is dry, apply the gold size sparingly all over the surfaces using a stiff paintbrush. Leave to dry; it will be ready for the next step when the surface is superficially dry but still slightly sticky when pressed with your finger.

1 Paint the box with gold acrylic paint to form the background.

3 Once the glue has dried, apply two coats of lacquer to the découpaged surface, allowing the first coat to dry before applying the second.

5 Next, apply a thin coat of the crackle glaze, making sure that you cover the whole surface. Fine cracks will begin to appear immediately, but allow the glaze to dry overnight to achieve the best results.

6 Dip a piece of kitchen paper into the raw umber oil paint and rub it gently all over the surface into the cracks. Leave for a few minutes, then wipe off the surplus and leave to dry. Once dry, apply six coats of polyurethane varnish, allowing each coat to dry before applying the next.

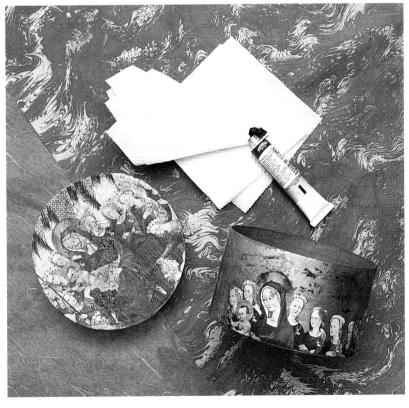

Edible Gifts

Food is supposed to be the way to a man's heart, but this does not only apply to men. Traditionally, because food is associated with nurturing, and because different types of food have been scarce in various cultures from time to time, a gift of food is an obvious and positive way of showing love.

As tastes vary so much, I have included both sweet and savoury food items. Homemade lemon curd is a real treat, and is also very easy to make. Most people like chocolates, so I have included a delicious recipe for truffles to tempt you.

Beautiful herbal oils and vinegars, as well as plump, sun-dried tomatoes, make great presents for vegetarian and meat-eating friends alike.

Another easy gift to make when going to a friend's for dinner or a weekend stay is shortbread. I have used biscuit cutters to make pretty shapes.

Of course, one of the fun things about making homemade food gifts is the many interesting and beautiful ways of packaging them – for example, using interestingly shaped jars and bottles, creating attractive lids, putting the gifts in baskets and so on. Some packaging ideas are demonstrated in this chapter, but these are only suggestions; there are so many more things you can do to dress up your food gifts in an attractive but simple manner.

Flavoured Oils & Vinegars

Infusing both oils and vinegars with herbs and spices is a great way to make a personalized gift for family and friends. Flowering herbs will make the oil or vinegar look pretty, as will colourful items such as red chillies and aromatic fruits such as lemons or limes. There are many different types of oil to choose from, but I find that sunflower oil is the best variety for infusing, as it is bland and readily absorbs the flavours of the added ingredients. When making flavoured vinegars, choose good-quality vinegar with an acetic acid content of 5 per cent or more. Be sure to sterilize the bottles before filling them.

You will need

Freshly picked herbs
Dried whole spices
Citrus fruits
Whole red chillies
Clear glass bottles of various shapes and sizes
Oil
Vinegar (malt or rice)

1 Prepare the herbs and spices first. Fresh herbs should be washed and then lightly dried on kitchen paper to remove any excess moisture. The dried spices should, ideally, be as fresh as possible.

2 Once you have prepared the herb and spice flavourings, insert them into the bottles. Add enough oil or vinegar to cover all the ingredients so mould cannot grow. Seal the bottles and leave for two weeks in a cool, dark place. During this time, the flavours will infuse.

Variations

ROSEMARY OIL
4 sprigs of fresh rosemary
Olive oil

CHILLI OIL
Red chillies
Black peppercorns
Sunflower oil

ORANGE OIL
Orange peel on a wooden skewer
Coriander
Sunflower oil

CORIANDER VINEGAR
Sprigs of fresh coriander
Vinegar

LEMON OIL
Lemon slices
Bay leaves
Black pepper
Sunflower oil

GARLIC OIL
Cloves of garlic on wooden sticks
Olive oil

GINGER SHERRY
Fresh root ginger
Sherry (in place of vinegar)

Attractive bottles filled with
oil or vinegar and sprigs of herbs make
sophisticated and delicious gifts.

Sun-dried Tomatoes in Olive Oil

Oil is perfect for preserving foods, and if the oil is a rich one – like extra virgin olive oil – it can give the food you are preserving a delicious flavour. Sun-dried tomatoes are particularly full of flavour when preserved in oil, and are easily available from supermarkets or health food shops. Soak them in boiling water, then repackage them with oil in large jars to make attractive and mouth-watering gifts.

You will need

Kitchen scales
25 g (1 oz) sun-dried tomatoes
Heatproof bowl
Boiling water
Sieve
Kitchen paper
Large glass jar and lid
2 bay leaves
50 ml (2 fl oz) white wine vinegar
100 ml (4 fl oz) extra virgin olive oil
Sticky label and raffia

2 Pack the jar with the tomatoes, tucking the bay leaves down the sides as you do so, but leaving about 2 cm (¾ in) of space at the top. Pour in the vinegar, then the olive oil, almost to the top of the jar, ensuring that the tomatoes are covered.

Seal the jar and keep in a dark, cool place for at least 2 weeks – this will give the flavours to sufficient time to combine.

1 Place the tomatoes in a bowl, cover with boiling water and leave for 5-10 minutes. Drain in a sieve and pat dry with kitchen paper.

3 To decorate, label the jar and tie a raffia bow around its neck.

Chocolate Truffles

*For all your friends and family with
a sweet tooth, truffles are the ideal gift.
Decorate them according to the occasion: egg shapes for Easter; mini-plum
pudding shapes for Christmas; heart shapes for St Valentine's Day
and numbers for birthdays.*

You will need

225 g (8 oz) digestive biscuits
Plastic bag
Rolling pin
100 g (4 oz) butter
Large tin of condensed milk
60 ml (4 tablespoons) of
cocoa powder
60 ml (4 tablespoons) of
desiccated coconut
Shallow dish
Knife
Greaseproof paper
Vermicelli, cocoa powder,
desiccated coconut or chopped
nuts for decoration
Small, fluted paper
confectionery cases

2 Melt the butter over a low heat, then add the crushed biscuits, condensed milk, cocoa powder and coconut. Mix thoroughly.

4 Roll the truffles in vermicelli, cocoa powder, coconut or nuts to decorate, then place in paper cases.

3 Spoon the mixture into a shallow dish, then spread it out evenly and place in the fridge to set. When the mixture is firm, cut it into small squares and roll each square into a ball between your palms. Place the balls on a sheet of greaseproof paper.

Variations

*To ring the changes,
you can add a few drops of
spirits or liqueur to the truffle
mixture. Depending on
individual preferences
you might like to add rum,
brandy, kirsch,
Cointreau or Drambuie.*

1 Place the digestives in a plastic bag, then use a rolling pin to crush them into crumbs.

Fresh Lemon Curd

A simple but mouthwatering food gift – a jar of fresh, homemade lemon curd is ideal with toast at breakfast or teatime, or used as an alternative to icing on a cake.

You will need

2 large lemons
Grater
2 bowls
Kitchen scales
150 g (6 oz) of caster sugar
Lemon squeezer
4 large eggs
Pan of simmering water
100 g (4 oz) unsalted butter
Knife
Wooden spoon
Sterilized jar and lid
Label
Pen

2 Whisk all four eggs into the lemon juice, then pour this over the sugar and lemon rind. Mix well, then place the bowl over a pan of simmering water and add the butter in little pieces. Stir until the butter has melted and the mixture has thickened – about 20 minutes.

1 Grate the rind off the lemons, place in a bowl, then add the sugar. Squeeze the juice of the lemons into a separate bowl.

3 Pour the mixture into a jar before it sets and allow it to cool before sealing. Label the jar and decorate it as you wish.

Shortbread

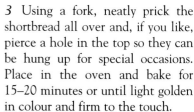

Shortbread is one of the first things you learn to cook in a home economics class at school, using the two, four, eight method. It is extremely simple to make, and you may well find that you already have the ingredients in your cupboard. So, for a quick, easy and delicious gift, shortbread is perfect.

You will need

Kitchen scales
50 g (2 oz) of caster sugar
100 g (4 oz) butter
100 g (4 oz) of plain flour
100 g (4 oz) of barley flour
or cornflour
Mixing bowl
Rolling pin
Novelty pastry cutters
Baking tray
Greaseproof paper
Fork

1 Set the oven at 170°C/325°F/gas mark 3. Place all the ingredients in a bowl and mix together using your fingertips – the mixture will look like fine breadcrumbs at first, but it will gradually begin to hold together. Once the mixture is in dough form, knead it into a smooth ball. Gently press and roll the dough into a round shape 1 cm (½ in) thick, keeping the edges smooth and free of cracks.

2 Cut out the shapes from the shortbread using the pastry cutters, and place these onto a baking tray lined with greaseproof paper.

3 Using a fork, neatly prick the shortbread all over and, if you like, pierce a hole in the top so they can be hung up for special occasions. Place in the oven and bake for 15–20 minutes or until light golden in colour and firm to the touch.

Variations

Choose packaging that is
appropriate to your chosen
shape. For example, the fish
on the right have been
arranged in a box to resemble
a tin of sardines.
For even jollier biscuits add a
few drops of bright food
colouring to the mixture.

Easter Presents

 Easter is a festival celebrated in many countries. It heralds the start of spring, bringing better weather and symbolizing rebirth and renewal.

It is not surprising, then, that the art of egg decoration in connection with Easter festivities is so widespread. This craft is practised in different forms in many countries, including Switzerland, Germany, the Netherlands and the Czech Republic.

In the Ukraine, Romania and Hungary the designs are painted on in hot wax before the eggs are put into a bath of cold-water dye. An easy decorating idea is to apply découpage or fabric scraps to an eggshell using glue and clear varnish. Alternatively, eggs can be dyed or painted a variey of colours, embellished with beads and braids, or etched or gilded.

In this chapter, you will discover many different examples of egg decoration. You will also learn techniques, such as how to create a hollow egg from papier mâché, and how it can be easily gilded or decorated and filled with homemade chocolate truffles.

As Easter is not complete without a bunny, I have created one complete with bloomers, a patchwork pocket and a carrot.

Gilded Papier Mâché Egg

Maybe geese only lay golden eggs in fairy stories, but you can certainly make one using paper, glue, a small piece of card and some gold leaf. This makes a great present for either an adult or a child, as it can be filled with different kinds of goodies, such as toys, sweets or miniature Easter eggs. For a particularly seasonal touch, fill the golden egg with egg-shaped chocolate truffles (see page 66).

You will need

Newspaper
Masking tape
Cling film
Wallpaper paste or wood glue,
slightly diluted with water
Scissors
Thin card
PVA glue
Paintbrushes
White emulsion paint
Quick-drying size or
glue/clear varnish mixture
(usually sold with gold leaf)
Gold leaf sheets
Soft brush

2 Rip newspaper into narrow strips and dip each strip into the wallpaper paste. Layer the strips over the cling film-covered mould until it is completely covered. Leave to dry. Add three more layers of paper and paste, leaving each layer to dry before adding the next.

3 When dry, remove the papier mâché shape from the mould where they are separated by the cling film. Repeat step 2 to make the second half of the eggshell.

Cut a length of card 1 cm (½ in) wide and glue this around the inner edge of one eggshell half to create a 'lip' that will eventually join the halves together. Paint a coat of white emulsion over both eggshell halves, inside and out.

4 Paint size or glue/varnish mixture on the outside of each shell half and allow to dry until it feels sticky. Keeping the backing paper on, smooth one sheet of gold leaf at a time over the size-covered eggshell with your fingers. Remove the backing paper once the leaf is securely attached. Repeat this process until both the eggshell halves are fully covered.

As the egg is oval-shaped, you will have to overlap the pieces of gold leaf to cover the whole surface. Rub off the excess with a soft brush or your fingertips.

1 Make a mould by carefully making a rounded, half-egg shape from scrunched newspaper, holding it together with masking tape. Add more pieces until you have a smooth, oval shape. (Alternatively, make the mould from plasticine or clay.) Cover the rounded side with cling film and secure it on the flat side with tape.

Easter Rabbit

This delightful Easter bunny is made from calico. She has long, floppy ears and is wearing red-checked bloomers under her smock. A contrasting patch pocket holds a felt carrot. This bunny makes a great gift, but for safety's sake, do make sure all the pieces are sewn on securely so that children can't pull anything off.

You will need

Tracing paper
Pencil
Scissors
Fabric marker
90 cm (1 yd) calico
Tape measure
20 cm (8 in) red-checked fabric
Sewing thread
Sewing machine
Needle
Pins
Soft-toy stuffing
40 cm (16 in) blue gingham
Fabric oddments for pocket
Optional star stamp
and fabric paint
Buttons for eyes
and decoration
Black embroidery thread
Small squares of orange
and green felt

1 Trace the templates on page 78, place on the calico and draw around them, making two head shapes, four ear shapes, two arms and two legs. Cut out each shape, ensuring the arms are the same shape and length as the leg pieces. Cut two calico rectangles 13 x 21 cm (5 x 8¼ in) for the upper body, and then two rectangles 13 x 10 cm (5 x 4 in) in red-checked fabric for the lower body. Then cut two rectangles of red-checked fabric 14 x 30 cm (5½ x 12 in) for the top half of the legs.

4 Tuck the open ends of the arms inside the body near the top, and sew into position while sewing up the side seams. Turn the body right side out, then fill with stuffing. Sew a loose running stitch around the head opening, gather it tightly and sew it on to the body.

2 With right sides facing, sew round the head, then turn right side out. Pin the checked upper leg pieces to the calico lower leg pieces, right sides together, and sew across the top. Open out, then fold lengthways, right sides together. Pin round the edges, leaving the top edge open, then sew round the foot and up the leg. Turn right side out. Sew round the arms in the same way and turn right side out. Sew the ear pieces together and turn right side out. Fill the head, arms and legs with stuffing. Press the ears flat with a hot iron.

5 Measure how long you want the dress to be, add a 2 cm (¾ in) seam allowance, then cut the blue fabric to this length. Pin the right sides together and sew up the back seam. Hem the top and bottom edges, then sew a patch pocket into the centre. Print a star on a spare piece of calico and sew this onto the pocket. Sew a line of running stitch 1 cm (⅜ in) from the top edge of the fabric. Fold the dress in half and cut two holes 1cm (⅜ in) below the running stitch on either side of the dress. Neaten the edges. Fit the dress over the rabbit's head and poke her arms through the armholes. Gather the dress to fit, then sew into position. Sew the button eyes into position, then stitch the rabbit's features with black thread.

3 Lay the checked fabric for the body on the lower half of the body pieces and sew them into place. With right sides facing, place the legs between the front and back of the body. Sew the legs into position along the bottom seam of the body.

6 Make the rabbit's carrot by sewing together two elongated triangular pieces of orange felt, then turning them inside out to hide the seams. Make the carrot top by cutting a piece of green felt 5 cm (2 in) square. Fringe the square 4 cm (1⅝ in) down one side. Roll the felt and sew together with a few stitches. Sew a line of running stitch around the top of the carrot, place the green felt in the centre, then pull the stitching to gather the top. Secure with a few hand stitches.

7 The rabbit's shoes are optional. To make them, trace around the lower part of the leg template, place on the red-checked fabric and cut out. Pin each shoe right sides together and sew around the curved edge. Hem the top edge and sew a button to the front. Slip the shoes over the feet and attach with a few stitches.

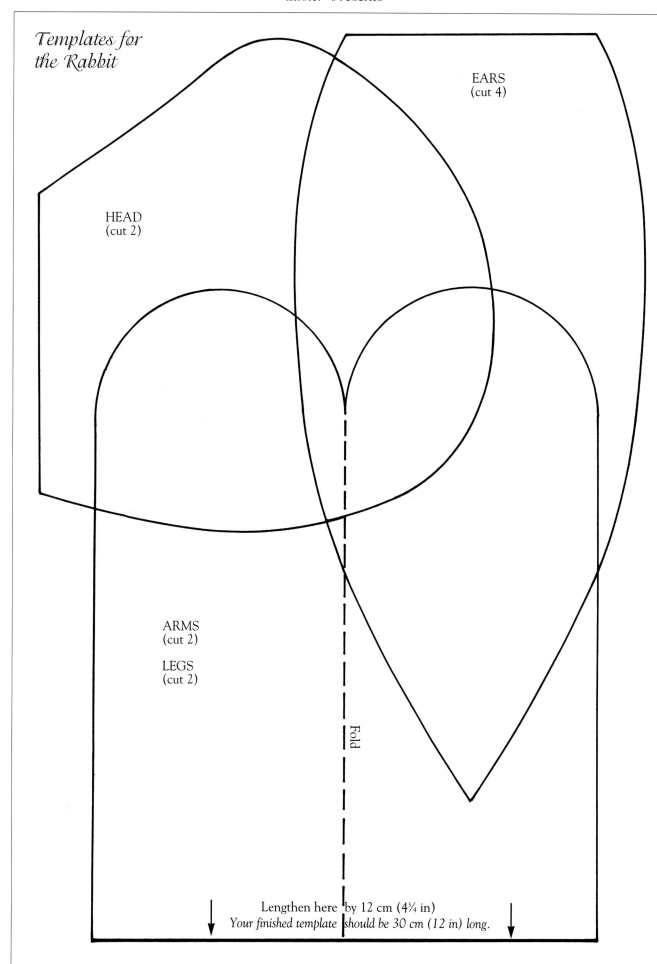

*Templates for
the Rabbit*

HEAD
(cut 2)

EARS
(cut 4)

ARMS
(cut 2)

LEGS
(cut 2)

Fold

Lengthen here by 12 cm (4¾ in)
Your finished template should be 30 cm (12 in) long.

Decorated Eggs

Eggs can be blown and then decorated, or they can be cooked and decorated at the same time. However, as cooked eggs cannot be kept, it is best to blow them if you are not intending to give them as edible presents. To blow an egg you must start by making small holes at each end of the shell. Hold the egg firmly and insert a pin first, then use a crosshead screwdriver or thin skewer to make the holes larger. Insert the screwdriver or skewer into one of the holes and give it a careful twist to break up the yolk. Hold the egg over a bowl and blow the contents out through the largest hole. Rinse the emptied shell with warm water until it is clean. Leave to dry in a warm place overnight.

You will need

FOR REAL EGGS
Eggs
Saucepan of cold water
Vinegar
Natural dyes (tea, onion skins, coffee, logwood, etc.)
or synthetic if preferred
Nylon stocking mesh
Small flowers or leaves
Pin and fine crosshead screw-driver or skewer for blown eggs

FOR ARTIFICIAL EGGS
Gold wax crayon
Gouache paints
(gold and other colours)
Polystyrene eggs
Lace, ribbon, beads, braid, sequins and gold crepe paper
Pins
Emulsion paints

Natural-dyed Eggs

Place several unblown eggs in a saucepan and cover with cold water. Add 30 ml or 2 tablespoons of vinegar (to give a richer colour), then add your chosen natural dye. (Logwood is usually available from chemists.) Bring the mixture to the boil slowly to avoid cracking the shells. Boil for 30 minutes, then turn off the heat and leave to cool.

When the water has cooled, remove the eggs using a wooden spoon or a metal spoon covered in nylon stocking mesh to prevent marking or scratching the shells. Leave to dry.

The eggs shown above were dyed in cochineal. They were then rubbed with a gold wax crayon to create a lustrous surface and painted with gold gouache paint.

Flower-dyed Eggs

I was taught this method of egg decoration by a Serbian girl many years ago. Although the method is simplicity itself, the results are really very interesting.

Collect some small flowers or leaves large enough to fit around an unblown egg. Moisten the eggs with water, then place the leaves or flowers on them. Cover with nylon stocking mesh and tie it securely with string to hold the plants in place. Colour the flower-wrapped eggs using natural dyes (see page 79), or synthetic dyes, if you prefer, following the instructions on the packet. When the dyeing process is complete, cut away the nylon mesh and peel off the leaves or flowers to reveal their outlines where the dye hasn't penetrated.

Hand-painted Eggs

Eggs can be decorated with many different materials, including lead pencil, felt-tip or pen and ink. The eggs shown here were dyed with cochineal, then rubbed with a gold wax crayon or decorated with gold gouache patterns.

Homemade Artificial Eggs

Eggs can be formed from many substances – wood, soap, plaster of Paris, wire, mesh, marble, sponge, salt dough, clay, fabric, topiary, cake, chocolate, marzipan, sugar, mousse, fondant – and most can be made relatively easily at home. For example, you can make Easter egg candles by melting some old candles and re-forming the wax into egg shapes. Alternatively, glass and plastic eggs can be bought ready-made in gift stores and then decorated at home.

You can decorate your artificial eggs, as I have done with the pretty wooden ones shown here, using a coat of gouache to give an overall background colour, then by creating a series of floral or geometric shapes from simple dot patterns. When the paint is dry, cover the egg completely with a coat of clear varnish.

Beaded Eggs

These eggs look like large duck eggs, but are in fact made of polystyrene. They are available by mail order (see Stockists, page 110), and can be decorated with old lace, ribbon, beads, braid, sequins and gold crepe paper, which are attached to the eggs with dressmaker's pins. The pins are dipped in glue, then pushed through the fabric or beads and into the polystyrene egg.

Emulsioned Eggs

Household emulsion can be mixed in many deep shades and used to paint eggs. The matt finish of the paint is particularly suitable for the eggs' surface. Those shown here look very modern and would make a great present for someone with minimalist taste.

Baby Gifts

The birth of a new baby is a wonderful excuse to give a present. I have tried to come up with gifts that are a little out of the ordinary, but are also easy to make.

The nursery bag can be used for toys, laundry, or all those items needed for nappy changing. I have chosen a country print and theme for the bag, but if you prefer, you can vary these with either pastels or bright primary colours.

Knitted hats and mittens are often given to babies and toddlers, as they are both useful and attractive handmade presents. I have included a fun design for a hat with ears and matching mittens that will delight small children.

A name plaque made from salt dough is a good personalized present for any age, from a tiny baby to an elderly aunt. This is a useful idea for those times when you can think of no other gift to give. It costs very little, since it uses only household ingredients.

Mobiles make great presents for babies, as newborns love looking at them. We have designed a mobile using small teddy bears which are readily available in toyshops and department stores. To make them look different, you can customize your bears using bits of ribbon, buttons and decorative trims.

Salt Dough Plaque

The salt dough plaques featured here have a simplicity reminiscent of Shaker design. The figures are minimal and the colours subdued, so the overall effect is subtle rather than brash. If you do not like this muted-colour palette, you could experiment with primary or brighter colours for a different effect. The best salt dough creations are left to dry out before baking, then baked at a very low temperature to protect against distortion.

You will need

FOR THE DOUGH
2 level mugs of plain white flour
1 level mug of finely ground salt
30 ml (12 fl oz) of lukewarm water

FOR THE PLAQUE
Rolling pin
Pastry cutter
Garlic press
Skewer
Paper clip
Baking tray
Paintbrush
White emulsion or gesso
Acrylic paints

1 To make the dough, mix the dry ingredients in a bowl, gradually adding enough water so that you can knead the mixture into a pliable ball. If the dough becomes too wet, add more flour. Knead it well before using. The more it is kneaded, the more pliable it becomes.

2 Roll out a piece of salt dough and cut out a circle with the pastry cutter. This is for the plaque. Make one figure at a time, rolling out one ball for the head and four long sausage shapes for the limbs. Then make triangular shapes for the bodies.

3 Mix some of the dough with a little water to form a paste and use this to stick the pieces to the plaque.

4 Squeeze some dough through the garlic press and stick it on to the heads of the figures to create hair. Use a skewer to mark the eyes and mouth, then make holes in the dough as decoration.

5 Make the name out of strands from the garlic press and place these on the plaque. Stick a paper-clip in the back of the plaque so it can be hung up. Leave to dry out overnight.

6 Place the plaque on a baking tray and bake in the oven at 130°C/ 250°F/gas mark ½ for about 1 hour. It is ready if it sounds hollow when tapped on the base. Leave to cool, then paint it with a coat of white emulsion or gesso. When this has dried, paint in the details using acrylics.

Variation

As an alternative, you can make small, free-standing Shaker-style figures as charming decorations.

Appliquéd Nursery Bag

*This bag is a wonderful present for someone
with a new baby. Instead of the usual primary or pastel
colours typically used for baby gifts, I have chosen multicoloured print fabrics. Alternatively,
you can collect old and faded or precious scraps of fabric to create a work of art.
In the past re-using materials was a necessity and nothing was wasted. Clothes were always
handed down, and when too ragged to be worn, were turned into rugs, quilts or appliqués.
If you do not wish to make the bag, the following steps can be used to decorate
a ready-made cotton drawstring bag.*

You will need

Calico fabric
Iron and ironing board
Tracing paper
Pencil
Sharp scissors
Fabric scraps
Pins
Needles
Tacking thread
Bright sewing thread
Embroidery thread
Flat linen buttons
Gingham fabric
*(the amount depends on the
size of bag you want to make)*
Sewing machine
Length of cord
Safety pin

1 Cut a strip of calico large enough to make a panel on the bag, and iron flat. Using the shapes in the picture above as a guide, make a template for the ones you want, adding a 5 mm (¼ in) seam allowance all round. Cut them out and pin to the fabric scraps.

2 Snip into the seam allowance a few times, discarding the template when you've finished cutting. Carefully fold the allowance under. This can be difficult, but the snipping helps ease the turns on corners and curves. Use a hot iron to press flat.

3 Place all the fabric shapes on the calico strip using the photo as a guide. Pin or tack into position, through their centres or around the edge, which is a little more secure. Using a needle and bright sewing thread, overstitch round the edge of the shapes. The stitches can be quite large, as this adds to the naive design. Remove the pins or tacking thread and press once more with a hot iron.

4 Use other embroidery stitches on the rest of the design: sew grass in long green stitches; make brightly coloured flowers and eyes from French knots.

5 Fold under the edges of the calico strip by 5 mm (¼ in) to neaten. Press flat with a hot iron. Thread a needle with a double thickness of brightly coloured thread. Decorate the edge of the strip with blanket stitch and sew flat linen buttons on the corners.

6 Now make the bag. Take a piece of gingham twice as wide as it is long, and cut it in two. Sew the appliqué strip by hand onto one piece of the fabric, somewhere near the bottom. Pin the bag right sides together, then sew the sides and bottom seam. On each side at the top, turn down 5 cm (2 in) of raw edge. Machine sew into place. To make the casing, turn the top edge under 4–5 cm (1½–2 in) and machine sew into place leaving a small gap for the cord. Thread the cord onto a safety pin and push through the casing. Undo the pin and knot the ends of the cord together to make the drawstring for your bag.

Star-struck Hat and Mittens

Designed by Zoë Mellor

*This hat and mittens set is not only
a lovely present but is also very practical.
As well as a having a set of false ears that will delight children, the hat is
designed so that the real ears of the baby or toddler are covered and kept warm.
The pattern is given in sizes for three age ranges: 12–24 months,
2–4 years and 5–7 years.*

You will need

100 (100:150)g main colour (M)
Aran-weight wool
Small amounts of 3 contrast
colours (A, B and C)
1 pair of 3¼ mm
and of 4 mm needles.

Tension

Hat
20 sts and 28 rows = 10 cm
(4 in) square over stocking stitch
using 4 mm needles

Mittens
22 sts and 30 rows = 10 cm
(4 in) square over stocking stitch
using 3¼ mm needles

Abbreviations

k = knit
p = purl
st(s) = stitch(es)
patt = pattern
foll = following
folls = follows
rib = on even number of sts,
  every row *k1p1* to end
rib = on odd number of sts,
  Row 1: *k1p1* to last st k1
  Row 2: k1 *k1 p1* to end
sl = slip next stitch
yb = yarn to back of work
yf = yarn to front of work
k2tog = knit next 2 sts together
p2tog = purl next two sts together

p2togb= purl next 2sts together
  through back of sts
p3tog=purl next 3sts together
psso= pass slipped stitch over
ml= pick up loop before next st
  and knit into the back of it.
$ = repeat instructions as per
  all previous text
stocking stitch= Row 1: knit
  Row 2: purl
*   * = repeat enclosed
  instructions number of times
  indicated
(:) = brackets refer to larger
  sizes. Where only one figure is
  given, this refers to all sizes.

Hat

Using 3¼ mm needles and A, cast on 131(139:147)sts, work as follows: **Row 1**: Using M, *k1p1* to last st, k1. **Row 2**: rib 25(27:29) *sl k2tog psso pl sl k2tog psso* rib 67(71:75). *   * again, rib 25(27:29). **Row 3**: rib 23(25:27) *p3tog k1 p3tog* rib 63(67:71) *   * again, rib 23 (25:27). **Row 4**: rib. **Row 5**: rib 21(23:25) *p3tog k1 p3tog* rib 59(63:67) * *again, rib 21 (23:25). **Row 6**: rib 19(21:23) *sl

k2tog psso pl sl k2tog psso* rib 55(59:63) *   * again, rib 19(21:23). **Row 7**: rib 17(19:21) *p3tog k1 p3tog* rib 51(55:59) *   * again, rib 17(19:21). **Row 8**: rib 20(22:24) yb sl yf turn; *sl rib 3 yb sl yf turn: sl rib 5 yb sl yf turn, sl rib 7 yb sl yf turn: sl rib 10 yb sl yf turn, sl rib 13 yb sl yf turn: sl rib 16 yb sl yf turn, sl rib 19 yb sl yf turn: sl rib 23 yb sl yf turn, sl rib 27 yb sl yf turn:

For sizes 2-4 and 5-7: sl rib 31 yb sl yf turn, sl rib 35 yb sl yf turn:*

For all sizes: sl rib 69(77:81) yb sl yf turn, work from * to * again, then sl rib to end. Change to 4 mm needles and stocking stitch, and work as follows: **Row 1**: k 8(11:13) *k2tog k 22(23:24)* 3 times, k2tog, k9(11:14) 87(95:103)sts. Work 17(17:19) more rows. Follow size instructions; decrease only rows given.

12-24 months: **Row 19**: *k4 k2tog k5* 7 times, k4 k2tog k4. **Row 22**: *p4 p2tog p4* 7 times, p4

p2 tog p3. **Row 25**: *k2 k2tog k2 sl k2 tog psso * 7 times, *k2 k2tog* twice. **Row 27**: *k1 k2tog k3* 8 times. **Row 28**: p2tog p1 *p2tog p3 * 7 times, p2tog. **Row 29**: k1* k2tog k1* 10 times. **Row 30**: p1* p2tog* 10 times.

2-4 years: **Row 19**: *k5 k2tog k5* 7 times, k5 k2tog k4. **Row 22**: *p4 p2tog p5* 7 times, p4 p2tog p4. **Row 25**: *k3 k2tog k5* 7 times, k3 k2tog k4. **Row 29**: *k2 k2tog k2 sl k2tog psso* 7 times,

k2 k2tog twice. **Row 31**: *k1 k2tog k3* 8 times. **Row 33**: *k2tog k3* 8 times. **Row 34**: p2tog p1 *p2tog p2* 6 times, p2tog p3. **Row 35**: k2tog *k2tog k1* 6 times, k2tog k2tog. **Row 36**: p1 *p2tog* 7 times.

5-7years: **Row 21**: *k5 k2tog k6* 7 times, k5 k2tog k5. **Row 24**: *p5 p2tog p5* 7 times, p5 p2tog p4. **Row 27**: * k3 k2tog k6* 7 times, k3 k2tog k5. **Row 30**: *p2tog p3* 15 times, p2tog p2. **Row 33**: k1

k2tog k6 7 times, k2tog k4. **Row 35**: *k2tog k5* 7 times, k2tog k4. **Row 37**: k2 *k2tog k1* 15 times. **Row 39**: k1 *k2 tog* 15 times, k1. **Row 40**: p1 *p2tog* 8 times.

All sizes: Run thread through remaining stitches and pull together; then fasten securely. Join the hat sides together and sew.

To make the ears
Using 4 mm needles and A, cast on 12sts. Work in stocking stitch. **Rows**

1-2: using A. **Rows 3-4**: using B. **Rows 5-6**: using C. **Rows 7-8**: using A. **Row 9**: using B, k2 sl k1 psso k4 k2tog k2. **Row 10**: using B. **Row 11**: using C, k2 sl kl psso k2 k2tog k2. **Row 12**: using C. **Row 13**: using A, k2 sl k1 psso k2tog k2. **Row 14**: using A. **Row 15**: using B, s1 k1 psso k2 k2tog. **Row 16**: using B, p2tog p2togb. **Row 17**: using B, k2tog, fasten off.
Make one more ear as above, then two more ears using M only.

For finishing: Place one plain ear and one striped ear with right sides together and sew around the edges, leaving the bottom edge open. Place the ears approximately 5 cm (2 in) apart and sew securely on to the hat.

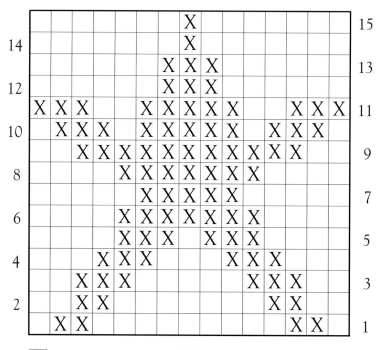

							X								15
							X								14
						X	X	X							13
						X	X	X							12
X	X	X			X	X	X	X	X			X	X	X	11
	X	X	X			X	X	X	X	X		X	X	X	10
		X	X	X	X	X	X	X	X	X	X				9
			X	X	X	X	X	X	X						8
				X	X	X	X	X							7
			X	X	X	X	X	X	X						6
			X	X	X			X	X	X					5
		X	X	X				X	X	X					4
	X	X	X							X	X	X			3
	X	X									X	X			2
X	X											X	X		1

☐ Main Colour   ⊠ Contrast Colour

Mittens

Cuff: Using 3¼ mm needles and M, cast on 29(33:38)sts and work two rows k1 p1 rib. Change to stocking stitch and work 0(2:4) rows. Change to C, work two rows. Change to B, work 2 rows. Change to A work 2 rows. Change to M work 1 row. Change to k1 pl rib and work 10(12:14) rows. Change to stocking stitch (starting with a knit row to reverse fabric), work 0(2:4) rows.

Shaping for thumb, right-hand mitten: **Row 1**: k15(17:19) m1 k1

(1:2) ml k13(15:17). **Row 2**: purl. **Row 3**: Start star k0(1:2); work Row 1 from star chart (15sts), k0(1:2) ml k3(3:4) ml k13(15:17). **Row 4**: p18(21:25), work Row 2 from star chart, p0(1:2). **Row 5**: k0(1:2), work Row 3 from star chart, k0(1:2) m1 k5(5:6) m1 k13(15:17). Continue as set, increasing 2sts on alt rows to completion of Row 10. **Row 11**: patt 26(28:31) turn: cast on 1st , p12(12:13) turn: cast on 1st, k13(13:14) 39(43:48)sts. On these 13(13:14)sts work 5(7:9) rows in stocking stitch.

Next row: k2tog twice, *sl k2tog psso*1(2:3) times, k2tog 3(2:1)times Break yarn, thread through sts and pull tight. Secure and sew thumb seam. With right side facing, rejoin yarn to base of thumb, pick up 3sts from base of thumb and complete Row 11. Work six more rows to complete the star, then work

further 1(3:5) rows.
Shape top: **Row 1**: Using M, k1 *sl k1 psso k10(12:14) k2tog k1*twice. **Row 2**: M, purl. **Row 3**: Using A, knit. **Row 4**: A, purl. **Row 5**: Using B, k1 *sl k1 psso k8(10:12) k2tog k1* twice. **Row 6**: B, purl. **Row 7**: Using C, k1 *sl k1 psso k6(8:10) k2tog k1*twice. **Row 8**: C, 12–24 months, purl, 2–4 (5–7)yrs, pl *p2tog p(6:8) p2togb pl* twice. **Row 9**: Using M, k1 *sl k1 psso k4(4:6) k2tog k1* twice; **Row 10**: M, p1*p2 tog p2(2:4) p2tog pl* twice. Cast off. $

Left-hand mitten: Make cuff* * as in right-hand mitten. Shape for thumb. **Row 1**: k13(15:17) m1 k1(1:2) m1 k15(17:19). **Row 2**: purl. **Row 3**: k13(15:17) m1 k3(3:4) m1 k0(1:2), work first row from star chart, k0(1:2). Continue as set, increasing 2sts on alt rows to completion of row 10. 39(43:48) sts. **Row 11**: k24(26:29) turn; cast on 1st, p12(12:13) turn; cast on 1st, k13(13:14) Work from $ to $ as on right-hand mitten.

Finishing: Join top and side seam, reversing fabric for cuff seam. Weave in any loose ends.

Circus Teddy Mobile

This gift is made with small, shop-bought teddy bears, which are then dressed enchantingly to look like circus entertainers and hung from embroidery thread above a small child's cot or crib. The mobile frame can be simply constructed by crossing two wire coathangers; alternatively, you can buy dowelling, paint it in bright colours, and use it to make a simple cross. Please note that this gift is for a young child to look at: it is not designed to be touched, as parts could be pulled off and eaten or swallowed.

You will need

Small teddy bears
2 pieces of dowelling or
2 wire coathangers
Thread
Tape measure
Remnants of broad ribbon,
fabric, leather or netting
Scissors
Needle
Pins
Sequins
Flat, round lid
Pencil
Fabric glue
Oddments of narrow ribbon
Gold braid and diamanté trim
Buttons
Assorted beads
Small, dyed feather

1 Make the frame by crossing the two pieces of dowelling in the centre, then binding them together with thread. You can also make a frame by tieing two wire coathangers together so that they form a cross.

2 To make clothes for the bear above, measure it around the middle and cut a piece of red satin ribbon three times the width you have measured. Fold the ribbon in half lengthways, wrong sides facing. Make a loop by sewing the ends together with a running stitch. Sew a line of running stitches along one edge of the loop and pull up the gathers. Put this 'skirt' round the bear's waist, pull tight and sew into position. Measure a piece of ribbon, fabric or leather that is large enough to go round the bear's body with an overlap at the front. Centre it in front of the bear, use pins to mark places for the armholes, then cut them out. Place this top on the bear with the opening to the back. Sew a green star sequin on the back to close the gap. Sew green star sequins randomly over the skirt. Cut a piece of green netting and tie this in a bow round the bear's head.

3 To make clothes for the bear on the left, cut three layers of net the same size as the red ribbon in step 2. Cut the first layer of net the same depth as the ribbon, the second layer 1cm (⅜ in) narrower and the third 1cm (⅜ in) narrower than the second. Sew the three layers of net together with running stitch, narrowest piece on top, then gather and attach to a narrow piece of ribbon wide enough to fit round the bear's waist: sew into place. Cut the waistcoat as in step 2 and decorate with rocaille and bugle beads. Sew a glittery headband from a length of braid to fit around the bear's head. Use glue to fix a purple feather on the back.

4 To make the clothes for the bear on the right, find a lid which will balance on top of the bear's head. Draw around the lid on the fabric and cut this circle out. Stick the fabric circle on top of the lid, then stick a narrow piece of ribbon around the edge. Cut another piece of narrow ribbon and stick it to the underside of the lid so that it can be tied under the bear's chin and thus keep the hat in position.

To make the trousers cut four pieces of ribbon long enough to reach from the bear's waist to his knees. Make one leg at a time: sew two pieces of ribbon together down their length and pin onto the side of the bear's waist. Do the same for the other leg. While the trousers are still pinned to the bear, sew the front seams and inside legs by hand. Remove the pins.

Make a waistcoat, as in step 2, but this time place the opening at the front and trim it with narrow gold braid. Thread a piece of diamanté onto a piece of grosgrain ribbon and place over the waistcoat. Sew the ribbon together at the back. Put the hat on the bear.

5 To make the clothes for the bear on the left, cut four pieces of wide grosgrain ribbon and make the trousers as above. Attach narrow ribbon from the front to the back of the trousers over the bear's shoulders. Sew bright buttons at the join. Make a collar by cutting a piece of ribbon three times the width of the bear's neck; sew running stitch along one long edge. Draw up the gathers and adjust to fit the bear's neck. Sew up the back seam. Cut a piece of very narrow ribbon for a headband and sew this around the bear's head.

Christmas Gifts

 Christmas is celebrated in many parts of the world, and is a special time for exchanging gifts. As many of the gift ideas in this book are suitable for giving at any time, this chapter concentrates on items specifically for Christmas.

There is a traditional wreath which can be as simple or as complex as you care to make it.

Pomanders are suitable presents for both men and women, they are easy and inexpensive to make, and give off a wonderful and long-lasting aroma.

For those who prefer an alternative to traditional Christmas decorations, or perhaps as a present for someone who does not have room for a Christmas tree, I have included a hanging spiral of vine twigs with its own decorations.

Christmas stockings are universally popular so basic instructions are given here togther with suggestions for innovative styles.

Most shop-bought fairies, stars or angels for the top of a Christmas tree tend to be very ornate, so I have created here a very simple design of an angel holding a felt heart.

Although swags look expensive and very elegant, they are nonetheless very easy to make and require very little skill. The instructions are given with clear, step-by-step illustrations so you can make your own decorative swags, using a combination of materials you have at home or those that are readily available during this season.

Christmas Wreath

A festive Christmas wreath is a welcoming sight which helps to lift the spirits on a cold, dark winter's night. Look out for holly, both the plain and variegated varieties; with luck, it may also be a good year for berries. Ivy and other evergreens make good wreaths, especially when decorated with fir cones and nuts. All wreaths start with a base or frame, which is sometimes meant to be visible and becomes part of the overall design. Frames can be made from scratch, but are usually inexpensive to buy. The base can be constructed from wire or wisteria vine or use a twig base for a more natural look. These can be bought ready-made very cheaply or you can shape them yourself. Small wires used for attaching items to wreaths are known as stub wires; these are available from florists.

You will need

Wisteria vine or twig base
Stub wires
Secateurs or pruning shears
Pieces of holly (with berries
if possible) and/or other
pieces of evergreen

2 Strip the leaves and berries off the lower holly stems. This will make it easier to assemble the wreath.

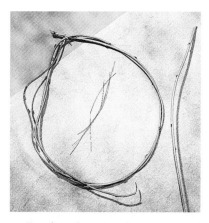

1 Bend and manipulate pieces of wisteria vine to form a circle. After the initial shape has been made, more pieces may be added to strengthen it. These can be twisted or wired into place.

3 Using stub wires, tie the stems of holly onto the ring or insert the holly between the pieces of twisted wisteria. Add bunches of holly facing in the same direction, overlapping each bunch as you work. Stand back and admire. If there are gaps, add single pieces of holly or berries.

Variations

A child's wreath can be made by decorating a vine or fake leaf wreath using a glue gun and old wooden toys or Christmas tree ornaments. This is a great way to use up decorations which have lost their hanging strings.
Another attractive variation is to make a wreath from a single colour, such as silver, gold or red.

Decorated Twig Spiral

*Vine and twig spirals can be bought
from shops ready-made and in various sizes.
These can then be decorated to suit any season, festive or otherwise.
A spiral can be made at home using any pliable twigs or vines – honeysuckle, wisteria
and grape are the easiest to come by, and are therefore the most commonly used.
Depending on the size you want the spiral to be, make a base from a length of wire
(coathanger wire will suffice), and twist it into a spiral shape.
Make sure that the twigs are bendy and pliable. If they aren't, soak them in water for a while.
Start with long twigs and bend them along the wire base, adding in other lengths as you
go and twisting them together (two pairs of hands will make this job a little easier).
Tie wire around the twigs at intervals to keep them bunched together.*

You will need

A twig or vine spiral
Gold mesh ribbon
Gold crepe paper
Gold ribbons
Polystyrene balls in
various sizes
Gold paper leaves
Gold thread
Glue

1 Cover some of the polystyrene balls evenly with the gold paper leaves, glueing them into position. Use a pin to attach the balls to lengths of gold thread.

2 Wrap the remaining balls in crepe paper as you would wrap sweets, then cover them in gold mesh ribbon and tie at both ends.

3 Glue gold thread to the top of the balls so they can be suspended.

4 Hang up the spiral and tie the small balls at the top and the larger ones further down.

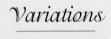

Variations

Keep the spiral simple and natural by suspending small cookie cutters from checked ribbons or dangling iced cookies with holes in them from delicate broderie anglaise or lace.

Pomander

Pomanders are an Elizabethan invention, initially used to mask evil smells. The original ones were small balls of gold, silver or ivory, beautifully filigreed and containing rare spices. They were hung on a chain and worn around the waist or neck. Modern pomanders can be made from any citrus fruit studded with cloves and cured in a mixture of spices.

You will need

Firm-skinned orange
Raffia
Cocktail stick
Whole, large-headed cloves
Brown paper bag
Ribbon
FOR THE CURING-
SPICE MIXTURE
100 g (4 oz)
powdered cinnamon
50 g (2 oz) powdered cloves
15 g (½ oz) powdered allspice
15 g (½ oz) powdered nutmeg
25 g (1 oz) orris root powder
(this makes enough to cure several pomanders)

2 Using the cocktail stick, pierce the orange in the places where you wish to insert cloves: they can be arranged on the fruit in patterns or placed randomly. Do not put them too close together as the fruit shrinks when it dries out. As you insert the cloves, the fruit should be held firmly without squeezing.

4 After a fortnight, remove the orange from the spices, shake off the excess powder and replace the raffia by a ribbon.

1 Tie a piece of raffia around the orange as shown in the picture. This will be replaced later by a ribbon.

3 Mix the spices together in a bowl or a paper bag and put the orange in the powder. Leave for two weeks, turning each day.

Variation

Gilded oranges look lovely in a basket arrangement. Take an unblemished orange and score several times right round the skin. Place in a very low oven to dry over 24 hours. When cool, paint with gold size and leave until just sticky. Cut gold leaf into strips, smooth it on to the orange using your fingers, and leave to dry. Brush off the excess gold with a soft brush, then rub with a harder brush for a distressed look.

Natural Fragrant Swag

A swag can look elegant and welcoming hung across a fireplace or above a doorway. If you want to achieve an especially festive look, gild the fruits before attaching them to the swag. The selection of objects placed on the swag is up to individual tastes, so if you have suitable items that are not mentioned in the list below, do feel free to use them.

You will need

*Tape measure
Chicken wire
Wire cutters
Florist's wire
Holly leaves, small fir
branches or other
evergreen leaves
Cinnamon sticks
Raffia
Oranges
Glue gun (optional)
Walnuts
Dried red chillies
Pine cones
Holly berries
Festive ribbons*

2 Insert the holly leaves and small fir branches into the tube, covering the wire and forming a base.

4 Cut the oranges into slices and dry in the oven on its lowest setting for 24 hours. Tie them into bundles with florist's wire. Allow the glue gun to heat up, then glue the walnuts, chillies, pine cones and holly berries randomly onto the chicken wire, making sure that one end does not look heavier than the other. Tie large bows of ribbon on each end of the swag and hang up.

5 Make some gilded oranges (see page 100) and attach in any spaces left by the larger objects.

3 Tie the cinnamon sticks into bundles of five or six with the raffia, and then tie the raffia ends to the chicken wire at various intervals and at various lengths.

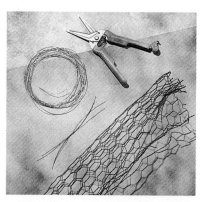

1 Measure the area where you wish to hang the swag and cut a piece of chicken wire a little longer than that and 18 cm (7 in) wide. Roll the wire into a tube and secure with florist's wire.

Variation

You can make a simple fragrant swag by threading dried oranges, groups of bay leaves and bunches of cinnamon sticks onto linen thread as shown here, or you could weave this through a larger swag, attaching the linen thread at certain points.

Christmas Tree Angel

A Christmas tree angel always has a special significance. What could be nicer, therefore, than making one to give as a Christmas present? The angel here is designed with a hollow skirt so that it can sit easily on the top of the tree. Apart from its head and hands, the rest of the angel is made from felt, which is easy to use as it can be glued rather than sewn and does not fray.

You will need

Tracing paper
Pencil
Scissors
White, pink and yellow
or orange felt
Small piece of calico or
unbleached cotton fabric
Gold thread
Needle
Wadding
Sewing machine
Fabric glue
Thick, blonde-coloured silk
Coloured pencils
Gold rocaille beads

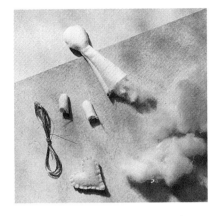

2 Take the two heart pieces and sew them together along the outside edge, again using the gold thread and a blanket stitch. Leaving a small opening at one end, stuff the heart with wadding, then close up the opening with blanket stitch.

Pin the head and neck pieces together with wrong sides facing. Machine stitch around the edge, leaving an opening at the bottom and a small seam allowance. Turn right side out, stuff with wadding and close up the opening.

Repeat this with the hands.

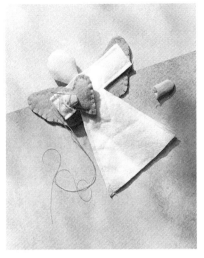

3 To make the gown, place the two pieces together and machine stitch along the sides of the gown and long edges of the sleeves, leaving gaps for the neck and hands. Sew the neck of the angel's head into the gown.

Sew the hands into the sleeve holes, then sew the heart to the hands, as if the angel is holding it. Sew wings to the back of the gown.

1 Make templates for the angel's gown, heart, wings, head and hands (see page 106). Use the templates to trace the gown onto white felt (x 2), the heart onto pink felt (x 2), the wings onto orange or yellow felt (x 2), the head and neck onto calico (x 2) and the hands on calico (x 4).

Take the two wing pieces and sew them together along the outside edge, using the gold thread and a blanket stitch. Sew random tacking stitches on the wings to add decoration.

4 Spread fabric glue on top of the head and lay rows of thick silk thread on it to make the hair. Draw in a mouth and eyes with the coloured pencils, using a pink pencil to colour in rosy cheeks.

To finish, sew gold bugle beads on the bottom of the angel's gown.

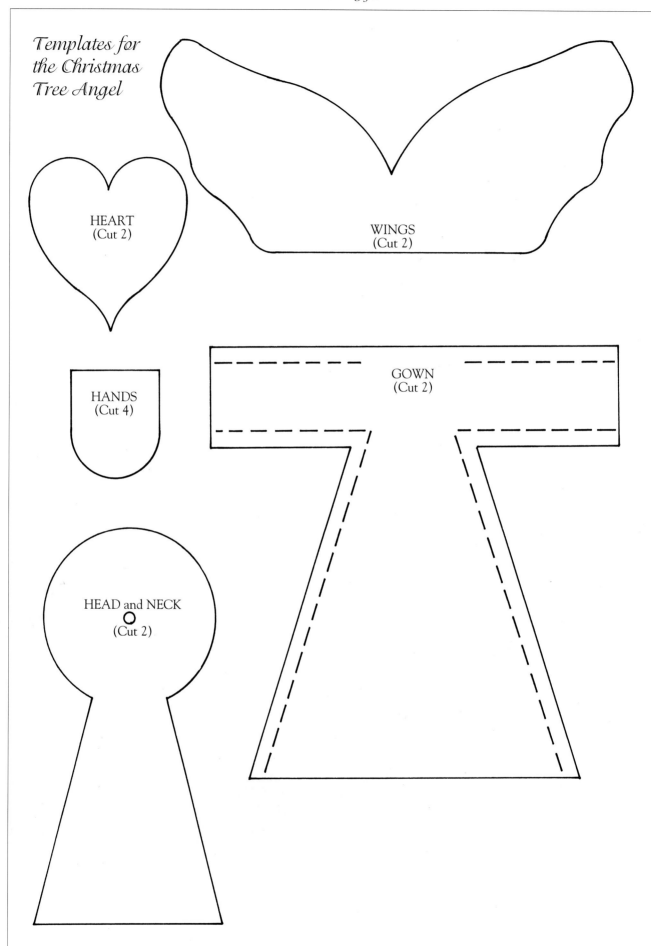

*Templates for
the Christmas
Tree Angel*

HEART
(Cut 2)

WINGS
(Cut 2)

HANDS
(Cut 4)

GOWN
(Cut 2)

HEAD and NECK
(Cut 2)

Christmas Stocking

A special Christmas stocking is a splendid gift.
You can give it an ethnic, adult or childlike look,
depending on the materials and images used. As with all the ideas in this book,
the stocking is made in the quickest way possible. Felt is the ideal material
as it is easy to work with and will not require frequent washing.

You will need

Paper
Pencil
Scissors
50 cm (½ yd) of red felt
Pinking shears
Dressmaker's pins
Contrasting colour threads
Scraps of green, purple
and yellow felt
Sewing machine
50 cm (½ yd) of
yellow rickrack

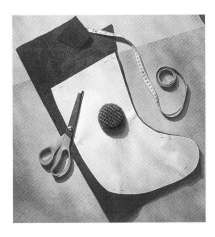

2 Fold the red felt in half and place the pattern on the top. Add 6 cm (2½ in) at the top for a cuff and cut out using pinking shears.

3 Cut out Christmas tree and star shapes from paper and pin these on different colours of felt. Cut around the shapes, then arrange and pin them onto the boot.

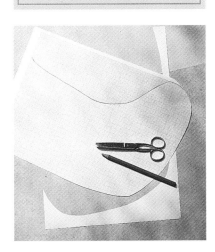

1 Using the photograph as a guide, draw a boot shape on paper, making sure that the foot slopes gently as this makes a better shape. Cut this out and use as your pattern.

5 Using pinking shears, cut out strips of purple felt approximately 1 cm (⅜ in) wide. Sew these strips onto the back of the red felt 5 mm (¼ in) from the edge, then sew a piece of yellow rickrack along the centre of the purple strip. Sew stars above the strip. Fold the cuff down 6 cm (2½ in) so that all the felt decoration shows on the same side. Pin the back and front of the boot together and sew around the edge, leaving the top open. Attach a rickrack loop to hang it up.

4 Sew the shapes onto the boot by machine or using running stitch.

Variations

Make a crazy patchwork boot from pieces of fabric ironed onto fusible webbing and decorated with diamanté, tassels or decorative items such as old Christmas decorations. Alternatively, make a simple appliqué design from scraps of fabric and attach bobbles, buttons or braid for decoration.

Stockists

United Kingdom

FRED ALDOUS LTD
(craft supplies)
37 Lever Street
Manchester M60 1UX
Tel: 0161 236 2477

CREATIVE BEADCRAFT
(beads and sequins)
Denmark Workshops
Sheepcote Dell Road
Beaumond End
Nr Amersham
Buckinghamshire HP7 ORX
Tel: 01494 715606

STEPHANIE DONALDSON
*(florists' sundries
and aromatic plants)*
Provenance Plants
1 Guessens Walk
Welwyn Garden City
Herts AL8 6QS
Tel: 01707 393 105

FINE FABRICS
*(fabrics, toy accessories,
needlecrafts)*
Magdalene Lane
Taunton
Somerset TA1 1SE
Tel: 01823 270986

HOMESTYLE
(lampshades)
Customer enquiries
Tel: 0800 996633

HOP SHOP
(lavender)
Castle Farm
Shoreham, Sevenoaks
Kent TN14 7UB
Tel: (01959) 523219

ZOË MELLOR
(children's hat and mittens)
26 Belvedere Terrace
Brighton
East Sussex
BN1 3AF
Tel/Fax: 01273 731 923

OFFRAY RIBBON
(ribbons)
Fir Tree Place
Church Road
Ashford
Middlesex TW15 2PH
Tel: 01784 247281

PRICES
*(candles and candle-
making supplies)*
110 York Road
London SW11 3RU
Tel: 0171 228 2001

RAINBOW RIBBONS
(ribbons, florists' sundries)
Unit 3, The Seed Bed Centre
Davidson Way
Romford
Essex RM7 OAZ
Tel: 01708 732621

ISABEL STANLEY
(heart brooch)
5 Herne Hill Mansions
London SE24 9NQ
Tel: 0171 326 4764

THE STITCHER'S MILL
(craft items via the Internet)
htt://rhwww.richuish.ac.uk/ext
/smill/home.htm

WORLD OF SEWING
(fabrics, ribbons, sewing supplies)
56–64 Camden Road
Tunbridge Wells
Kent TN1 2QP
Tel: 01892 533188

United States

AMSTERDAM ART
1013 University Avenue
Berkeley, CA 94710
Tel: 415 548 9663

SAM FLAX
111 8th Avenue
New York, NY 10011
Tel: 212 620 3060

SAX ARTS & CRAFTS
PO Box 51700
New Berlin, WI 53151
Tel: 414 784 6880

South Africa

CRAFTY SUPPLIES
32 Main Road
Claremont Cape
Tel: 021 610 286

HEALTH & HERB CENTRE
78217 Sandton City
Sandton 2146
Tel: 011 783 7906

New Zealand

BRIAR ROSE HERBS LTD
1/14 Greenmount Drive
East Tamaki
Tel: 09 274 7733

GORDON HARRIS
4 Gillies Avenue
Newmarket
Auckland
Tel: 520 4466

Australia

HANDWORKS SUPPLIES
121 Commercial Road
South Yarra
VIC 3141
Tel: 03 820 8399

HERBY'S HERB FARM
662 Manly Road
Manly
QLD 4179
Tel: 07 390 7220

Acknowledgements

The author and the publishers would like to thank the following people for all their help in making this book:

Homestyle for supplying lamp shades and bases; Hop Farm for supplying lavender; Fred Aldous for general craft materials, including leaves, stamens, polystyrene eggs and balls; Isabel Stanley for the brooch; Zoë Mellor for the hat and mittens; Creative Beadcraft for beads and sequins; Offray Ribbon for the ribbons; Prices for candles and terracotta pots with relief motifs; Labeena Ishaque, my brilliant assistant, who has styled this book beautifully and made many of the projects; Jon Bouchier for taking such wonderful photos; and Pippa Rubinstein, who invited me to write it.

Index